thelwell
annual
1980
CW01666062
thelwell
£1·85

Whether he's coming . . .

CONTENTS

. . . or going . . .

WORLD & WHITMAN

Published in Great Britain by World Distributors (Manchester) Limited, A Pentos Company, P.O. Box 111, 12 Lever Street, Manchester M60 1TS.
Printed in Belgium   SBN 7235 6566 X

. . . a pony will always be your very special four-footed friend.

WELCOME TO THE WORLD OF THELWELL

Welcome to the world of Thelwell. It is a wonderfully bright and happy world to explore, with all manner of unexpected and intriguing discoveries to be made along the way.

Our annual is a book about ponies, and about the people who love ponies. So if you're already a confirmed 'pony person' you might just find *yourself* popping up on our pages, or someone who bears you a very striking resemblance, at least.

But don't worry if you're a complete novice in this special world, and can't tell a martingale from a nose-bag. All you really need is a love of animals and of the countryside, and a strong sense of fun. If you qualify in these categories you'll love this book.

MEET THELWELL

Norman Thelwell is a cartoonist of quite exceptional talent. His work covers many subjects, but it is in country matters that he truly excels. He works in a studio overlooking the River Test in Hampshire, and his hobbies are painting and fishing.

Thelwell books are popular all over the world and have been translated many times, proving once more that humour is indeed the universal language.

MEET PENELOPE

As you browse through the pages of this book you'll have plenty of time to get to know Penelope. You could say that Penelope is a graduate of Norman Thelwell's own particular riding academy, and she has now set herself up as an instructress to others. Penelope has plenty to say about ponies. She teaches us, for instance, that they are really just like people, with their own little quirks, and their own funny little ways. They have their feelings, they can be offended or pleased, and they are quick to let us know their views. Here Penelope is giving us a particularly good example of a pony making his point.

ACQUIRING A PONY IS NOT QUITE SO EASY AS IT SOUNDS

HOW TO GET A PONY

YOU WILL LEARN A LOT BY LOOKING AT HIS TEETH

Finding your ideal first pony can be a tricky business, fraught with many hazards. Is this one tall enough? Is that one *really* only four years old? And does that one over there have to keep stamping his feet up and down in that silly way, or is he just being awkward? Nine times out of ten you'll discover, the answer to that last one is straightforward enough: he is just being awkward. But don't despair! For those brave few who stay the course and eventually win the approval of a four-legged friend, there's a grand future in store. It will be *nothing* but a smooth partnership of superb horsemanship and tremendous fun. What's that? Oh, the bruises . . . Well, who's counting a bruise or two here and there? And here? And there . . .?

YOU WON'T FIND YOUR PERFECT PONY STRAIGHT AWAY – BUT SOONER OR LATER

HE'LL FIND YOU

A CHRISTMAS SURPRISE

Of course there is always the possibility that someone will have done all the hard work for you, and you will receive your pony as a super Christmas surprise. In this case, there are one or two points to be noted. Number One, he won't want any holly garlanded round his neck. This is inclined to be itchy for him, and he can't reach his neck too well with his hind hooves. Number Two involves his feed, and the fact that however much you would like to draw him into the family Christmas, he really isn't that keen on turkey. Thirdly, remember that when the family settles round the TV set to watch the late-night film, he honestly would prefer to be in his stable. He's probably seen it before, anyway. To those generous folk who are giving the pony, it is sufficient to add that gift-wrapping this particular Christmas box is not generally a great success.

LEARNING TO RIDE

Learning to ride is exciting, exhilarating, and enjoyable. It is also painful from time to time. If you are either 1) 'a natural' or 2) very lucky, it won't take you many lessons to get the hang of sitting astride your pony's back, and maybe staying there for a minute or two, if he's feeling generous. Be prepared for the odd fall, and should you by any chance see the suspicion of a grin creeping round your pony's mouth, just tell yourself that you are probably imagining it.

IT IS A GOOD IDEA TO START BY LEARNING HOW TO MOUNT YOUR PONY

THE CORRECT SITTING POSITION MUST BE MASTERED

GRIP WILL IMPROVE
WITH EXPERIENCE

AND BALANCE
WITH PRACTICE

**TALK TO YOUR PONY –
HE WILL KNOW WHAT YOU MEAN**

THE JOYS OF THE COUNTRYSIDE

The countryside holds many joys for the young pony rider. On horseback one has the opportunity to see its beauty in new and inspiring ways. Dangling from the branches of a majestic oak, for instance, affords a unique bird's eye view which must be seen to be appreciated. Unasked, your pony is quite likely to help you up into this comfortable position. Then again, if he should suddenly spot something of interest, which he feels you should see, he might well stop dead in his tracks, without warning, to be sure you don't miss it. At times like these a firm hand on the reins can have you over his head and on the ground in next to no time. Or, ever thoughtful, he may choose to help you down from the saddle in an even more decisive way. A third possibility remains. It is just possible that your pony will decide that today is a day for resting, and quiet contemplation of the peaceful rural scene. If this is the case he will make himself comfortable, and you may as well follow suit. Until he's good and ready, you see, he won't be budged.

PONY PURSUITS

You and your pony will be able to take part in all manner of enjoyable pursuits.

You will be able to show your pony at the local agricultural show. He may not win a prize himself, but he will no doubt enjoy the day, and will find his own special way of showing his appreciation of the other prizewinners' exhibits.

The day of your first gymkhana will come. It will be a proud day for you if he proves himself to be the lively chap you always knew he was. Try to make sure, though, that he has some vague idea of just what it is he's supposed to be jumping.

This is without a doubt the finest way to enjoy the hunt, particularly for the fox. Highly recommended!

POINTS OF A RIDER

This is a beginner's guide to some of the most notable points of a rider. As your career in riding progresses you will no doubt be able to add some more of your own, for instance Areas Most Often Bruised, and Toes Most Often Trodden On (By Pony).

Penelope

IN THE OLD DAYS THEY USED TO RIDE SIDE-SADDLE. LIKE THIS!
WHATEVER FOR?
IT'S MORE LADY-LIKE!

THIS QUIET COUNTRY LIFE IS DOING YOU NO GOOD, LAZY BONES! I'M TAKING YOU OUT FOR A BIT OF ROAD-WORK! GETTING YOU INTO SOME HEAVY TRAFFIC WILL WAKEN YOU UP A BIT!
ZZZ
ZZZ

YOU'RE GETTING NO MORE CHOCOLATE, NO MORE PONY NUTS, NO MORE CAKE
YOU'RE GETTING NO MORE APPLES, NO MORE CARROTS, NO MORE SUGAR LUMPS
YOU'RE GETTING NOTHING! DO YOU HEAR? NOTHING! 'TILL YOU CONVINCE ME THAT YOU DESERVE IT!
I'M CONVINCED! I'M CONVINCED!

THERE YOU ARE! THAT'S YOUR RATION!
HE NEVER PUTS OFF 'TILL TOMORROW ANYTHING HE CAN EAT TO-DAY!

ALL RIGHT! ALL RIGHT! HAVE IT YOUR OWN WAY
GO IN THE CAR!

WERE YOU DISAPPOINTED, PENELOPE, WHEN KIPPER ONLY CAME THIRD IN THE SHOW JUMPING?
NO! I THINK HE DID WELL WHEN YOU CONSIDER THAT HE ALWAYS STARTS OFF WITH A HANDICAP OF FOUR FAULTS!
WHICH FOUR FAULTS?
HIS LEGS!

WHAT TO WEAR

Here are some tips for the well-groomed equestrian, or equestrienne, and his or her pony.

A SMART TURNOUT IS EXTREMELY IMPORTANT . . .

A RIDER'S ABILITY CAN USUALLY BE JUDGED

FROM HER APPEARANCE.

THERE IS NO POINT IN BEING WELL GROOMED YOURSELF, HOWEVER,

UNLESS YOU ARE PREPARED TO MAKE YOUR PONY . . .

. . . LOOK THE SAME.

ROOMY JODHPURS ARE ADVISABLE . . .

AND A HARD HAT IS A MUST . . .

ELABORATE WHIPS
IMPRESS NOBODY –
BUT REMEMBER . . .

THE MOST ESSENTIAL ITEM

IN A RIDER'S WARDROBE

IS A GOOD PAIR OF BOOTS.

WAY OUT WEST

THE WESTERN HORSEMAN

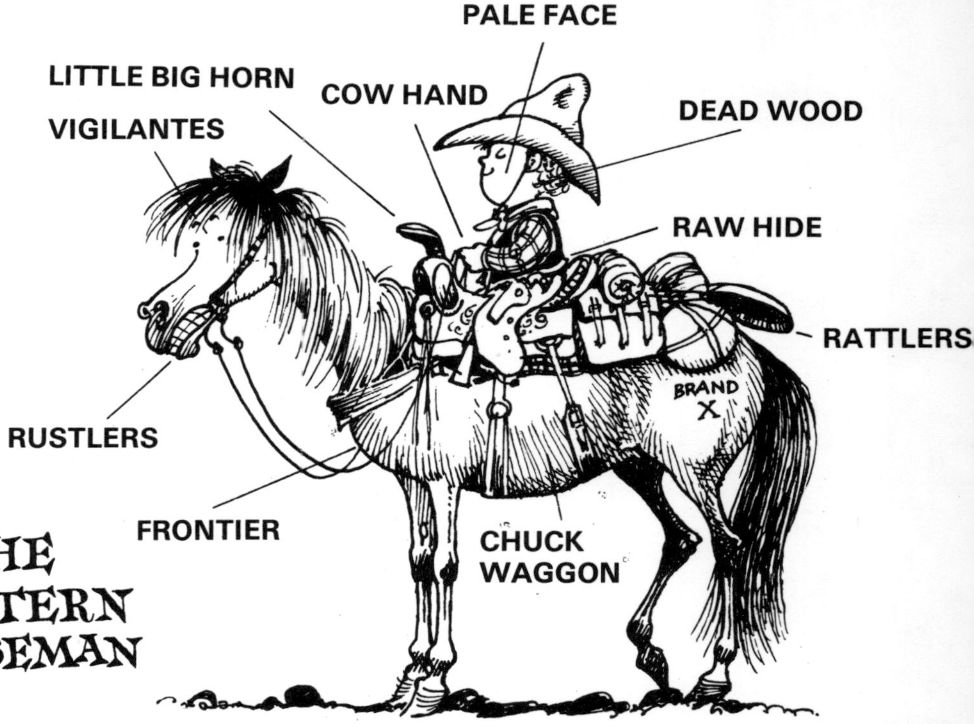

WESTERN TALK

Have you ever wondered just what the cowboys mean when they use those quaint old Western terms? Well, here are some possible interpretations of just two of them . . .

LOOKING DOWN THE BARREL OF A COLT

GET ALONG LITTLE DOGIE

HOW TO CROSS WATER

DO NOT TRY TO FORCE HIM INTO
THE WATER AGAINST HIS WILL

HE WILL GO IN
WHEN HE IS READY

DO NOT DISMOUNT AND
LEAD HIM FROM IN FRONT

HE IS LIKELY TO CLIMB ON TO
ANYTHING THAT LOOKS SOLID

WESTERN HORSES

THE MUSTANG

KNOWN THE WORLD OVER FOR HIS UNIQUE CONTRIBUTION TO THE MOTION PICTURE INDUSTRY, THIS LOVABLE HORSE HAS APPEARED IN MORE FILMS THAN BILLY-THE-KID

THE AMERICAN SADDLE HORSE

FAMOUS FOR HIS ABILITY TO EXECUTE AN ASTONISHING VARIETY OF SPECTACULAR GAITS

SCHOOLING

Your pony's schooling is vital to his development. You may find that it adds something to yours, too . . .

A HAPPY PONY THINKS OF YOU AS HIS BEST FRIEND

SO NEVER LOSE YOUR TEMPER OVER SOME LITTLE MISTAKE

HE MUST BE TAUGHT TO STAND CORRECTLY –

– TO BE LED WITHOUT FUSS

AND TO MOVE OFF PROMPTLY, WHEN ORDERED TO DO SO.

BUT HAVE SOME TIT-BIT HANDY FOR WHEN HE DOES WELL

HE WILL QUICKLY GET USED TO HAVING HIS BRIDLE PUT ON –

MASTERY IS ACHIEVED BY SUBTLETY . . .

. . . NOT BY ABUSE

BUT YOU SHOULD PUT SMALLER WEIGHTS ON HIS BACK BEFORE ATTEMPTING TO MOUNT HIM YOURSELF

BUT AT LEAST TWO PEOPLE MAY BE NECESSARY TO WORK HIM ON THE LUNGE REIN

PONIES ARE NATURAL JUMPERS

BUT DON'T EXPECT MIRACLES TOO EARLY

ENDLESS PATIENCE IS REQUIRED –

AND ABSOLUTE AUTHORITY MUST BE MAINTAINED

ONCE YOU HAVE GAINED YOUR PONY'S RESPECT – HALF THE BATTLE IS WON

Penelope

START

SOME PEOPLE ARE MYSTIFIED BY THE EVER INCREASING INTEREST IN HORSE RIDING!

THE EXPLANATION'S QUITE SIMPLE REALLY— AFTER ALL....
... IN THESE TIMES OF CHANGE AND UNCERTAINTY.....
WE ALL NEED SOMETHING TO HOLD ON TO!

DON'T LET HIM CARRY ON LIKE THAT, PENELOPE
SHOW HIM WHO'S MASTER
HE ALREADY KNOWS

IF YOU EVER LOST KIPPER, PENELOPE, WOULD YOU GET ANOTHER PONY?
NO! I COULD NEVER DO THAT, I'M AFRAID!

WHY NOT? YOU MIGHT GET ANOTHER ONE EXACTLY LIKE HIM!

THAT'S WHAT I'M AFRAID OF!

IF YOU CAN READ THIS NOTICE YOU'LL PROBABLY GET KICKED

CARE OF YOUR PONY

Follow these simple guidelines for a healthy, happy pony.

"DON'T JUST SIT THERE, DEAR – HURRY HOME BEFORE HE CATCHES A CHILL."

IT IS UNKIND TO RIDE YOUR PONY TOO FAST –

INSUFFICIENT EXERCISE, HOWEVER, CAN LEAD TO EXCESSIVE FAT . . .

SO GIVE HIM A GOOD LIVELY TROT EVERY DAY

THE RESULT WILL ASTONISH YOU.

NEGLECTING YOUR PONY'S COAT IS A SERIOUS MATTER . . .

. . . WHICH CANNOT FAIL . . .

. . . TO CAUSE TROUBLE

IF FLIES BOTHER HIM IN HOT WEATHER . . .

TIE A SPRIG OF ELDER TO HIS BROW BAND . . .

HE WILL FIND IT A GREAT RELIEF

YOUR PONY'S SHOES SHOULD BE CHECKED REGULARLY . . .

NEGLECT OF THIS SIMPLE PRECAUTION . . .

CAN LEAD TO SORE FEET.

YOU MUST LEARN TO
RECOGNISE SIGNS
THAT YOUR PONY
IS OFF COLOUR –

ROARING MAY INDICATE WIND TROUBLES . . .

. . . AND KICKING
MAY MEAN A SORE SPOT . . .

YOU WILL KNOW WHEN IT'S TIME
TO CALL FOR THE VET.

IN PREPARATION

Once you have mastered the basics of riding you will begin to start looking forward to your first gymkhana. As any experienced rider will tell you, it is important to prepare your pony well for this big event. The next three pages show preparation in progress: though the progress, you may note, is definitely of a slowish variety.

WE HAVE LIFT-OFF

A good approach to a jump is vital, and so is a good landing. Both these can be learnt, and both improve with practice. Here we see a group of would-be Horsewomen of the Year attempting to master both these tricky skills with the aid of some ingenious devices. As you will note, however, it is not always sensible to trust these new-fangled ideas too implicitly.

THE WATER JUMP

This is an unusually challenging jump which requires skills of a very particular kind. You will be able to guess that the pupils are beginners, thus they have felt the need to take certain precautionary measures against the very specific hazard which this jump presents.

TRANSPORT TROUBLES

Important as it is to concentrate on acquiring the skills you will need *in* the arena, it is also necessary to spend a certain amount of time practising those you will need before you actually arrive there. Getting your pony into his travelling-box can be as simple as opening it and watching him walk happily up the ramp. On the other hand, it can be an afternoon's work – *hard* work! If this is the case the end result is likely to be a great expenditure on sugar lumps, frayed tempers and harrassed expressions all round for the two-footed participants, and much sly smirking from our four-footed friends, who generally brace themselves firmly, and simply refuse to be budged. The ensuing chaos is graphically captured here, and if you think it's exaggerated, well, just wait till you try it . . .

BUCKING AND BOLTING

Bucking and bolting are two common problems with which every horseman has to cope.

THIS IS BOLTING

THESE ARE
BUCKING

AND THIS IS
BEING AWARE
OF THE BULL

THE RODEO

Following on from our interest in bucking, this picture shows it being used to spectacular effect in the popular sport of rodeo. Unbroken horses are used for this sport, and they readily co-operate, seeming to fling themselves into it with real enthusiasm. Could it be that they know this is just about the only chance they'll get of actually being *encouraged* to throw their riders?

GROOMING

Grooming should be approached methodically, and with the help of experts. It is quite an art . . .

MAKE SURE YOUR PONY IS SECURELY TIED

BEGIN BY REMOVING ALL SURPLUS MUD

USE THE BODY BRUSH VIGOROUSLY – HE WILL ENJOY IT

GET HIS TAIL WELL INTO THE BUCKET WHEN SHAMPOOING

AND BEWARE
OF WASHING HIS
MANE JUST
BEFORE A SHOW

BUT NEVER
CLIP HIM YOURSELF
UNLESS YOU ARE
AN EXPERT

HOLIDAY TIME CAMPING

Even the most dedicated rider needs a holiday sometimes, and as a general rule 'horsey' folk tend to choose lively holidays where they can enjoy themselves in the great outdoors. Camping is popular – and deservedly so. The joys of pitching your simple tent in a sweet-smelling

meadow are hard to beat. Friendly farm animals will come to give you their own special kind of welcome, and you can get in a little tree-climbing to keep you in trim. Camping holidays certainly do guarantee a whole load of fun. And they guarantee something else too . . .

Wherever you go on a camping holiday, and at whatever time of the year, you can be just *sure* that it will rain.

SAILING

"Oh, a life on the ocean wave!" Keen sailors will tell you there's nothing to beat a holiday afloat, and they're quick to reel off all the attractions of such a venture. There's the soft lapping of gentle waves, for instance. And even if the odd gigantic breaker should happen to swamp and capsize your little dinghy every now and then, well, what's a drop of water between friends?

FISHING

To angling enthusiasts the delights of fishing are supreme. Imagine the joy of landing your first tin can, old boot, or whatever other item of river refuse you might be lucky enough to hook. Baked in the oven in a delicious sauce, and served with French fries and peas, there's really nothing to match the subtle aroma and flavour of an old boot. One thing which you will have to bear in mind if you take up angling is that fish are inclined to be cunning and remarkably elusive creatures at times – times when you're fishing, that is. Most of the traditional pleasures of angling are illustrated here, but if these aren't enough to tempt you, just think of the fame you'll achieve as a storyteller on your return home. "Yes, it really was *this* big," your tales will begin.

YOUR PONY'S HEALTH

The following notes on the health of your pony should be self-explanatory. (Explaining them to the pony might be the hard part.)

IF YOU THINK YOUR PONY IS AILING

MAKE HIM WARM AND COMFORTABLE

COLDS CAN BE RELIEVED BY INHALING EUCALYPTUS

AND COUGHS BY SMEARING THE BACK OF THE TONGUE WITH PASTE

SYMPATHETIC NURSING
WILL WORK WONDERS

AND YOU
WILL KNOW
IT HAS ALL
BEEN WORTH
IT WHEN HE'S UP
AND ABOUT AGAIN

Penelope

"COME ALONG GIRLS.
PLAYTIME'S OVER."

"WHAT A SHAME!
THERE GOES HER EGG AND SPOON."

IT LOOKED LIKE BEING A GLORIOUS CLEAR ROUND!
THE CROWD WAS ON ITS FEET CHEERING US TO THE ECHO! KIPPER WAS GOING LIKE A BOMB!
I REALLY THOUGHT I WAS GOING TO WIN THE CUP THIS YEAR, FIONA!
THEN WE CAME TO THE FIRST FENCE!

I HATE HAIR-WASHING NIGHT, MAGNUS! IT'S A DREADFUL CHORE!
I HATE IT! DO YOU HEAR? I HATE IT!
HOT WATER! SHAMPOO! ALL THE RINSING DRYING, BRUSHING, COMBING...
THE MESS AND MUDDLE! ALL THAT CLEARING UP! AND THEN NEXT MORNING...
...I CAN'T DO A THING WITH IT!

I LOST THE CHAMPION JUMPER'S CUP AGAIN! AND ALL BECAUSE OF A SINGLE REFUSAL!
WHAT FANTASTIC BAD LUCK!
WHAT HAPPENED EXACTLY?
HE REFUSED TO GO INTO THE ARENA!

HE'S THE ONLY PONY I KNOW WHO INSISTS ON ADDING INSULT TO INJURY!

SAFETY PRECAUTIONS

Where ponies are concerned, you just *can't* take too many precautions . . .

"WHAT HAVE YOU DONE WITH HER THIS TIME?"

ALL ROAD SIGNS MUST BE STRICTLY OBEYED

AND ALL HAND SIGNALS CORRECTLY GIVEN.

SOME RIDERS LIKE TO HAVE A LOT OF BANDAGES ON THEIR HORSES

THIS IS NOT ALWAYS AS POINTLESS . . . .

. . . AS IT MAY APPEAR.

NEVER TRY OUT NOVEL WAYS OF GETTING INTO THE SADDLE

YOU'LL ENJOY QUITE ENOUGH VARIETY –

– GETTING OUT OF IT

NEVER SHOUT 'GEE UP'

. . . . WHEN TEACHER IS MOUNTING

IF ACCIDENTS ARE LIKELY TO OCCUR . . .

. . . AVOID WORRY . . .

. . . BY MAKING SURE THAT THERE IS A QUALIFIED VET IN ATTENDANCE

ALWAYS EXAMINE FENCES CAREFULLY BEFORE JUMPING

THIS WILL ENABLE YOU TO BE READY . . .

FOR AN EMERGENCY.

SOME OBSERVATIONS

"REMEMBER WHAT I TOLD YOU GIRLS, NEVER LET HIM SEE YOU'RE AFRAID."

DO NOT EXPECT HIM TO BE ABLE TO READ YOUR MIND

SHOW HIM EXACTLY WHAT YOU WOULD LIKE HIM TO DO . . .

"DON'T BE SO MEAN, GEORGINA – LET CHRISTABEL HAVE A TURN."

HE'LL BE VERY HAPPY TO OBLIGE YOU.

YOU MAY FIND THAT THERE IS MORE THAN ONE WAY OF WINNING A CUP . . .

SO IF ANY OBSTACLE SHOULD CAUSE HIM TROUBLE . . .

. . . TAKE HIM BACK . . .

IT CAN BE A RISKY TO BUY A PONY FROM A PUBLIC AUCTION

. . . . REASSURE HIM . . .

. . . AND MAKE HIM DO IT AGAIN.

MAKE SURE YOU KNOW HOW TO PICK UP HIS FOOT . . .

MAY CAUSE YOU INCONVENIENCE

LACK OF ABILITY IN THIS DIRECTION

REMEMBER THAT THE RULES OF THE ROAD APPLY TO YOU . . .

AS WELL AS TO OTHER ROAD USERS

BREEDS

Let's take a new look at Britain's pony breeds.

THE NEW FOREST PONY LIVES ALMOST EXCLUSIVELY ON A DIET OF LETTUCE, CUCUMBER AND FISH PASTE SANDWICHES

THE WELSH MOUNTAIN – OUR MOST BEAUTIFUL NATIVE BREED – IS INCLINED TO BE A TRIFLE WIDE IN THE BARREL

THE ANCIENT CONNEMARA WAS HANGING ABOUT GALWAY BAY LONG BEFORE THE SONGWRITERS GOT THERE

THE SHETLAND – WHICH IS THE WORLD'S SMALLEST BREED . . .

. . . IS RESPECTED BY ALL WHO KNOW HORSEFLESH

FELL & DALE CAN CARRY
PRODIGIOUS WEIGHTS WITH EASE

THE HIGHLAND IS USED
BY SPORTSMEN TO CARRY
THEIR 'BAG' DOWN THE
MOUNTAINS

THE EXMOOR IS MEALY-MOUTHED

OWING TO THE HARSHNESS
OF ITS ENVIRONMENT
THE DARTMOOR HAS
BECOME TOUGH & HARDY

Penelope

BLOOD GROUP
O RH. Neg

I'M SO HUNGRY I COULD EAT A HORSE!
I SAY THINGS WITHOUT THINKING

SQUEAK
SQUEAK
SQUEAK
SQUEAK
SQUEAK